TAKING JASON TO GRANDMA'S

Written by Margaret Mooney
Illustrated by Robert van der Wielen

Sunday

Dear Tony,

Would you like to come to stay with me?

Love from Grandma

Monday

Dear Grandma,

I would like to come to stay
with you.
I can come on Saturday.

Love from Tony

Tuesday

Dear Tony,

I am glad you are coming
to stay on Saturday.
Would you like to bring a friend
with you?

Love from Grandma

Wednesday

Dear Grandma,

I would like to bring Jason with me.
He lives next door.
You will like Jason.

Love from Tony

Thursday

Dear Tony,

I am glad you are bringing Jason.
I hope his mother won't miss him
too much.

Love from Grandma

Friday

Dear Grandma,

Mom will bring us
at two o'clock tomorrow.

Love from Tony